PRO WRESTLING'S GREATEST
RIVALRIES

BY MATT SCHEFF

SportsZone

An Imprint of Abdo Publishing
abdopublishing.com

abdopublishing.com

Published by Abdo Publishing, a division of ABDO, PO Box 398166, Minneapolis, Minnesota
55439. Copyright © 2017 by Abdo Consulting Group, Inc. International copyrights reserved in all
countries. No part of this book may be reproduced in any form without written permission from
the publisher. SportsZone™ is a trademark and logo of Abdo Publishing.

Printed in the United States of America, North Mankato, Minnesota
092016
012017

Cover Photo: Jonathan Bachman/WWE/AP Images
Interior Photos: Jonathan Bachman/WWE/AP Images, 1, 4-5, 15; Matt Roberts/ZumaPress, Inc./
Alamy, 6-7; George Napolitano/Getty Images, 8; Scott Gardner/Toronto Star/Getty Images, 9;
Alexandre Pona/CityFiles/Icon SMI/Newscom, 10; Mike Lano Photography/wrealano@aol.com,
11, 16, 20-21; ZumaPress/Icon SMI, 12; Bruce Bennett/Getty Images, 13; Don Feria/WWE/AP
Images, 14, 17; K. Mazurr/Wirelmage/Getty Images, 18-19; Richard Drew/AP Images, 22; Yukio
Hiraku/AFLO/Newscom, 23; Matt Roberts/ZumaPress/Newscom, 24; Russell Turiak/Getty Images,
25; Carlos Osorio/AP Images, 26-27; s_bukley/Newscom, 28-29

Editor: Patrick Donnelly
Series Designer: Laura Polzin

Publisher's Cataloging-in-Publication Data
Names: Scheff, Matt, author.
Title: Pro wrestling's greatest rivalries / by Matt Scheff.
Description: Minneapolis, MN : Abdo Publishing, 2017. | Series: Pro wrestling's
    greatest | Includes bibliographical references and index.
Identifiers: LCCN 2016945680 | ISBN 9781680784978 (lib. bdg.) |
    ISBN 9781680798258 (ebook)
Subjects: LCSH: Wrestling--Juvenile literature. | Sports rivalries--Juvenile
    literature.
Classification: DDC 796.812--dc23
LC record available at http://lccn.loc.gov/2016945680

TABLE OF CONTENTS

Brock Lesnar was in trouble.

Lesnar was facing his biggest rival, The Undertaker, at WrestleMania 30 in 2014. The Undertaker had won 21 straight WrestleMania matches. The Undertaker grabbed a stunned Lesnar and drove his head into the mat in a crushing piledriver.

The referee counted, "One! Two! . . . " But Lesnar shocked the crowd by kicking out of the pin.

The Undertaker, *top*, had the upper hand on Brock Lesnar at WrestleMania 30.

The Undertaker tried again. This time, Lesnar reversed the move. He slammed The Undertaker to the mat and covered him. The referee counted to three. It was over! The crowd couldn't believe it. Lesnar had ended his rival's historic winning streak.

Rivalries are part of what drives the action in World Wrestling Entertainment (WWE). Fans love a tough, back-and-forth battle. Rivalries can stretch over years and even decades. They're a huge part of what keeps fans coming back for more.

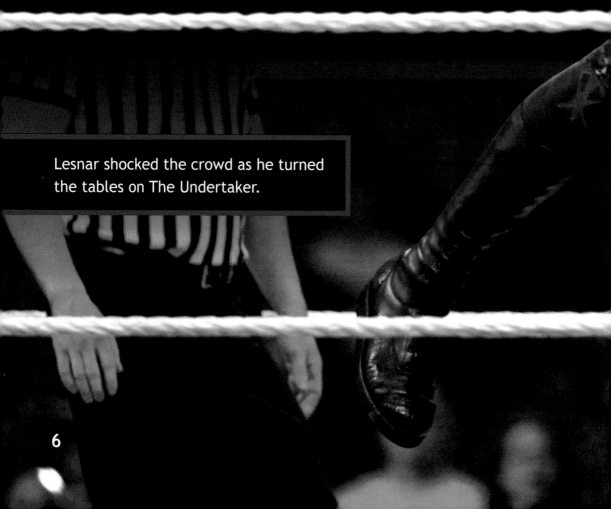

Lesnar shocked the crowd as he turned the tables on The Undertaker.

TEN

HULK HOGAN VS. RANDY SAVAGE

Two of the biggest WWE stars of the 1980s had an up-and-down relationship. Hulk Hogan and "Macho Man" Randy Savage were, at times, best friends. They banded together to form the Mega Powers. The friendship didn't last, however. The partners turned into bitter rivals. Savage's on-screen girlfriend, Elizabeth, was often at the center of their feud.

Randy Savage, *left*, and Hulk Hogan were partners at times, enemies at others.

Savage has the upper hand on Hogan.

NINE

THE UNDERTAKER VS. BROCK LESNAR

The feud between The Undertaker and Brock Lesnar didn't start with a major story line. It was just two guys who didn't like each other. The rivalry kept going when Lesnar left WWE to pursue a career in mixed martial arts. The Undertaker even appeared at some of those matches to glare at Lesnar.

The rivals met one last time in October 2015. Lesnar got the last laugh. He beat The Undertaker in a bloody steel cage match.

The Undertaker wasn't a fan of Lesnar, inside or outside the ring.

Brock Lesnar holds his
championship belt.

11

EIGHT

RIC FLAIR vs. RICKY "THE DRAGON" STEAMBOAT

This rivalry of the 1970s and 1980s was good vs. evil. Ricky "The Dragon" Steamboat was the all-around good guy, also called a *babyface* or simply *face*. Flair was the villain—also called the *heel*. The two battled each other as many as 2,000 times.

One of their best matches was at the Chi-Town Rumble in 1989. Steamboat pinned Flair to win the National Wrestling Alliance (NWA) heavyweight title.

Ric Flair

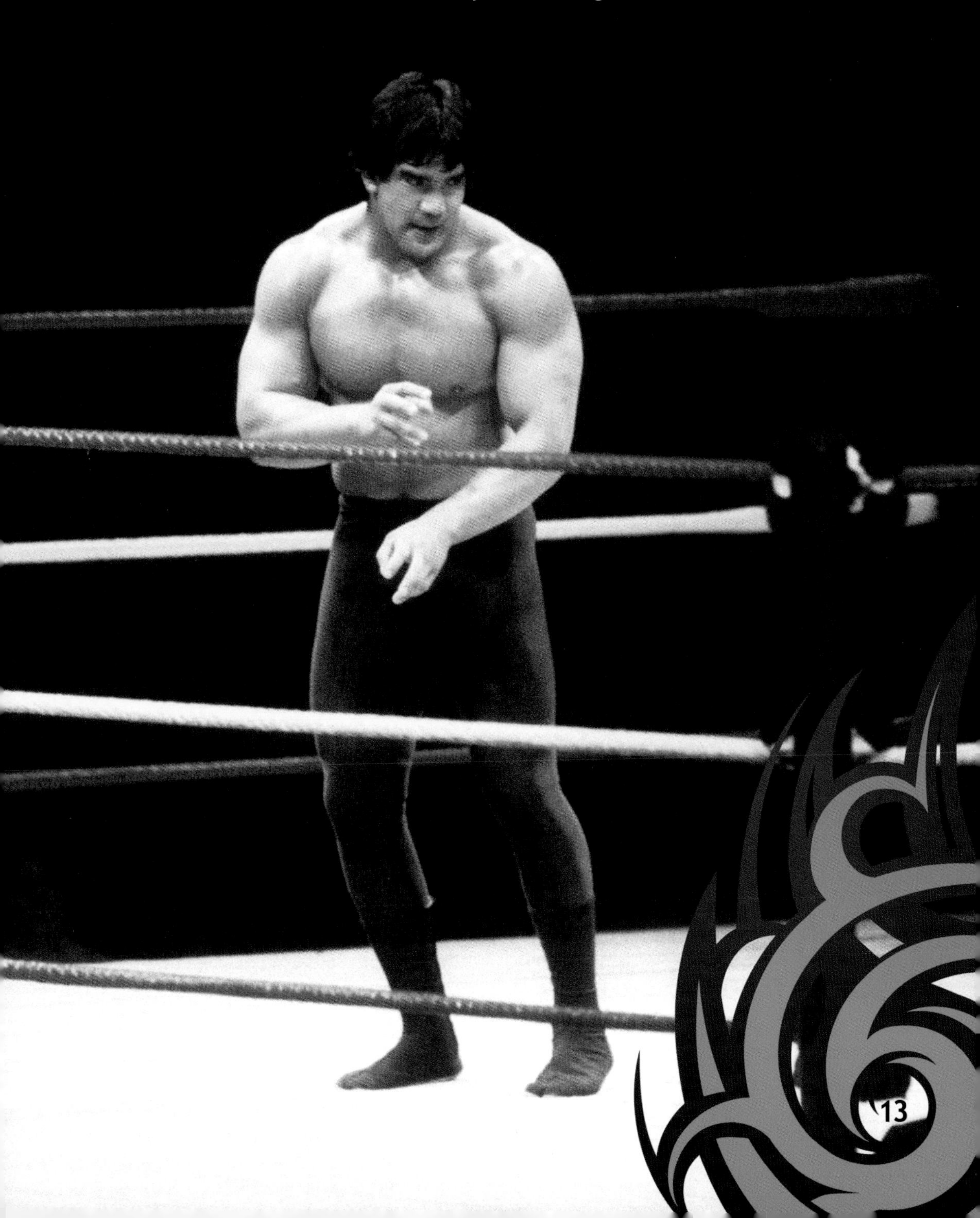

SEVEN

JOHN CENA vs. RANDY ORTON

John Cena and Randy Orton have a lot in common. They are superb athletes. Both started in WWE in 2002. Before long, they stood as the two dominant forces in WWE.

A rivalry bloomed. They took turns beating each other for the WWE championship in a series of heated matches. Orton, the heel, even once dragged Cena's dad out of the audience and kicked him in the head!

John Cena has taken the WWE belt from Randy Orton numerous times.

Orton and Cena had many memorable battles.

The Rock stands over a fallen Triple H.

CHANGING NAMES

When their rivalry started, both wrestlers used different names. The Rock was Rocky Maivia. Triple H was Hunter Hearst Helmsley. Both later shortened their names. Name changes remain a common part of pro wrestling today.

SIX

THE ROCK vs. TRIPLE H

The late 1990s and early 2000s were a time called the "Attitude Era" in WWE. Two of the biggest stars of the era were The Rock and Triple H. Both men were big, strong, and skilled. For half a decade, they battled for the WWE Intercontinental Championship.

The rivalry really took off in 1998. The two men fought in a brutal ladder match at SummerSlam. Triple H climbed the ladder to claim the belt.

A classic staredown: The Rock, *left*, and Triple H

FIVE

THE UNDERTAKER vs. KANE

The Undertaker was a rising WWE star in 1997. That's when a new force showed up: his long-lost brother, Kane. It was not a happy reunion. The Undertaker had once tried to kill his brother. Kane was back for revenge.

The two soon joined forces to form the Brothers of Destruction. But the partnership didn't last. The two massive fighters remained among the most bitter rivals in wrestling history.

The Undertaker, *left*, and Kane squared off at WrestleMania 20.

The Rock, *left*, and "Stone Cold" Steve Austin had many memorable matches.

THE VALET

Early in WWE history, many wrestlers brought female partners to the ring with them. These "valets" sometimes got involved in matches. They hid weapons, distracted referees and opponents, and fueled rivalries. Elizabeth was among the most famous valets in wrestling history.

FOUR

"STONE COLD" STEVE AUSTIN vs. THE ROCK

In the late 1990s, fans couldn't get enough of "Stone Cold" Steve Austin vs. The Rock. It started in 1997 when The Rock stole the Intercontinental belt from Austin. For the next four years, the men constantly clashed.

The two men faced off one last time in 2003 at WrestleMania 19. Many fans considered The Rock's victory there to be the end of an era for WWE.

21

THREE

HULK HOGAN VS. ANDRE THE GIANT

In the 1980s, Hulk Hogan and Andre the Giant were larger than life. For much of the decade, they were tight allies. But the friends began to feud in 1987. Andre the Giant demanded a title match at WrestleMania 3. Hogan managed to defend his title. Poor health soon forced Andre to quit wrestling, ending a great rivalry.

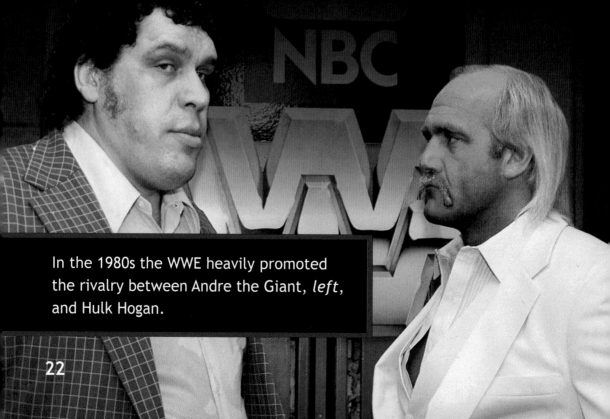

In the 1980s the WWE heavily promoted the rivalry between Andre the Giant, *left*, and Hulk Hogan.

Not many wrestlers could handle the 7-foot-4-inch Andre the Giant.

HOLLYWOOD STARS

Like many wrestlers, both Hogan and Andre the Giant took up acting. Andre the Giant made fans with his role in *The Princess Bride* (1987). Hogan starred in many films, including *Suburban Commando* (1991).

TWO

BRET HART vs. SHAWN MICHAELS

In the late 1980s, Shawn Michaels was part of an up-and-coming team, the Rockers. They challenged The Hart Foundation, led by Bret Hart, for the tag team title.

Both men moved on to singles wrestling. The rivalry went with them. Their high-flying matches thrilled fans and put them among the WWE's biggest stars.

Shawn Michaels

"STONE COLD" STEVE AUSTIN vs. VINCE MCMAHON

In the late 1990s, Vince McMahon was a WWE commentator. He stayed on the sidelines. But McMahon couldn't stand Steve Austin. McMahon did all he could to strip Austin of his title belt. Week after week, Austin managed to outwit McMahon. Fans loved it.

"Stone Cold" Steve Austin plays referee as Donald Trump, *left*, and Bobby Lashley prepare to shave Vince McMahon's head at WrestleMania 23.

Austin, *left*, and McMahon joined forces outside the ring to promote WWE.

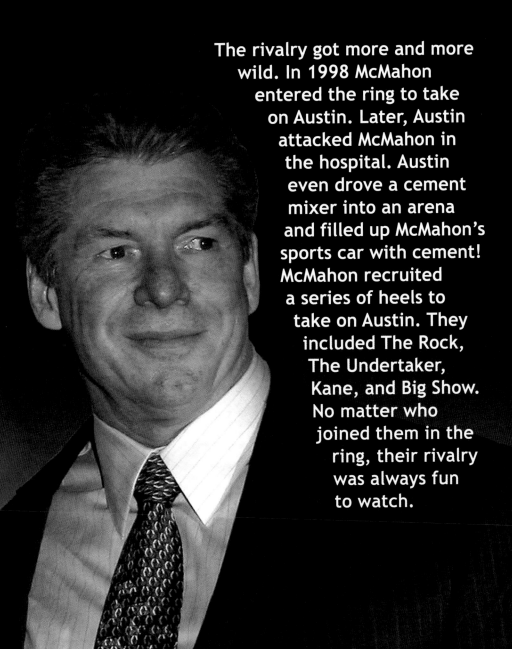

The rivalry got more and more
wild. In 1998 McMahon
entered the ring to take
on Austin. Later, Austin
attacked McMahon in
the hospital. Austin
even drove a cement
mixer into an arena
and filled up McMahon's
sports car with cement!
McMahon recruited
a series of heels to
take on Austin. They
included The Rock,
The Undertaker,
Kane, and Big Show.
No matter who
joined them in the
ring, their rivalry
was always fun
to watch.

GLOSSARY

ATTITUDE ERA
A period in pro wrestling during the late 1990s and early 2000s; the Attitude Era marked a period when pro wrestling marketed itself more strongly to adults.

BABYFACE
A wrestler seen as a good guy; also called a face.

COMMENTATOR
A television announcer for a wrestling match or other sporting event.

FEUD
A bitter disagreement between two or more people.

HEEL
A wrestler seen as a villain.

LADDER MATCH
A match in which the first wrestler to climb a ladder and grab a belt earns the championship.

PILEDRIVER
A move in which a wrestler grabs his opponent, turns him upside down, and drops into a seated or kneeling position.

PIN
A victory in which a wrestler holds his opponent's shoulders to the mat.

RIVALRY
A long-standing, intense, and often emotional competition between two people or teams.

FOR MORE INFORMATION

BOOKS

Kortemeier, Todd. *Superstars of WWE*. Mankato, MN: Amicus High Interest, 2016.

Scheff, Matt. *Pro Wrestling's Greatest Matches*. Minneapolis, MN: Abdo Publishing, 2017.

Scheff, Matt. *Randy Orton*. Minneapolis, MN: Abdo Publishing, 2014.

WEBSITES

To learn more about pro wrestling, visit booklinks.abdopublishing.com. These links are routinely monitored and updated to provide the most current information available.

INDEX

ABOUT THE AUTHOR

Matt Scheff is an artist and author living in Alaska. He enjoys mountain climbing, deep-sea fishing, and curling up with his two Siberian huskies to watch wrestling.